For Oscar and Ralph

The author would like to thank BMW Plant Oxford;
Dr. Charles Ambrose at Charles Trent Limited, Vehicle Dismantlers, Poole, UK;
and Mr. Paul Rutherford, Chief Vehicle Advisor, for their help and advice.

Henry Holt and Company, LLC
Publishers since 1866
175 Fifth Avenue
New York, New York 10010
www.HenryHoltKids.com

Distributed in Canada by H. B. Fenn and Company Ltd.
First published in the United States in 2008 by Henry Holt and Company, LLC
Originally published in England in a slightly different form in 2007 by Frances Lincoln Limited

Library of Congress Control Number: 2007926781

ISBN-13: 978-0-8050-8747-5
ISBN-10: 0-8050-8747-8
The illustrations in this book are collages of torn paper.

First American Edition—2008
Printed in Singapore

1 3 5 7 9 10 8 6 4 2

The Life of a
CAR

Susan Steggall

HENRY HOLT AND COMPANY • NEW YORK

Build the car.

Deliver the car.

Sell the car.

Drive the car.

Fill the car.

Wash the car.

Fix the car.

Tow the car.

Strip the car.

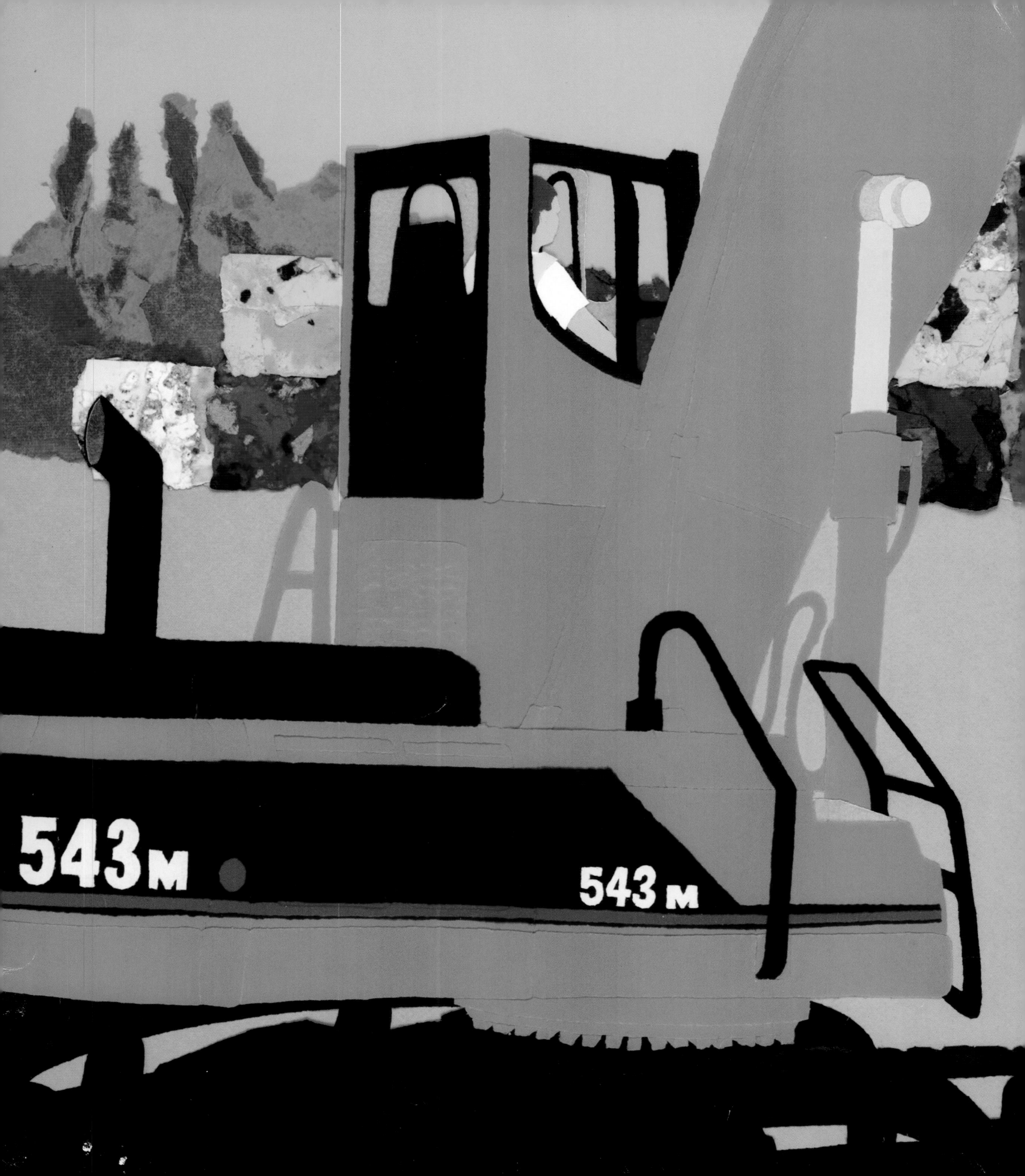
543м
543 м

Crush the car.

Recycle the car.

Then start again
and build a new one!